NILANJANA

A TERRIFIC TRUE STORY OF A SINGLE INDIAN WOMAN, WHO UNDERGOES A LOT IN HER LIFE.

SOUMILI PAUL

ISBN 979-888555574-6

I WOULD LIKE TO THANK ALL THE BEAUTIFUL SINGLE WOMEN
AROUND ME WHO SETS AN EXAMPLE FOR THE YOUNG FIGHTERS.

HERE, I WOULD ALSO LIKE TO THANK NILANJANA DEVI FOR LETTING
ME WRITE HER STORY.

Contents

Foreword

'THE BEST I READ TODAY' BY MY HUSBAND
'GO ON LIKE THIS' BY NILANJANA DEVI

Preface

THE STORY IS ABOUT NILANJANA AND HER STRUGGLES THROUGHT HER LIFE.

Acknowledgements

I WOULD LOVE TO THANK MY HUSBAND AND GOD FOR ALWAYS BEING WITH ME IN MY DIFFICULT TIMES AND MOST IMPORTANTLY TO HAVE FAITH IN ME!

IT IS BECAUSE OF YOU THAT I AM HERE.

Prologue

So, later the evening of 2021 Laxmi Puja I sat down to write the story as I couldn't believe the terrible incidents happened to Niju.

I WOULD LIKE TO SAY THAT NILANJANA WILL ALWAYS BE SPECIAL FOR
MY WRITING CAREER.

I

THE STORY BEGINS FROM THE EARLY YEARS OF THE 60'S WHEN NILANJANA (NIJU) WAS BORN. SHE WAS BORN IN A VILLAGE OF BONGAON (BANGLADESH BORDER). SHE WAS HER PARENTS SECOND DAUGHTER AND THIRD CHILD; SHE HAD 8 SIBLINGS. NIJU'S FATHER'S NAME WAS TRILOKESH AND HE WAS A FARMER, SO HE HAD A TOUGH LIFE AFTER A WHOLE DAY OF HARD WORK HE COULD BARELY BE SEEN GIVING COMPANY TO THE KIDS. HER MOTHER WAS NAINA DEVI WHO WAS A VERY DEDICATED HOUSE WIFE AND A SUPPORT SYSTEM TO HIS DAD. THE FAMILY WERE VERY PARTRIARCHAL BY NATURE.

BASICALLY, IN THESE KIND OF FAMILIES WHEN A WOMAN GETS PREGNANT EVERYBODY AROUND KEEPS TELLING HER THAT IT HAS TO BE A BOY, A BOY WILL MULTIPLE THE PRIDE OF THE FAMILY AFTERALL AND A GIRL WILL ONLY BRING UP MISERIES. IN THAT WAY NIJU'S MOTHER HAS ALSO BEING THE VICTIM OF SUCH UTTERANCE FOR ATLEAST MORE THAN 4 TIMES IN HER LIFE BUT SHE IS RELAXED AS SHE HAS BORE 3 HEALTHY SONS. ACCORDING TO NIJU, A COUPLE SHOULD BE VERY POSSESSIVE AND SENSITIVE ABOUT THEI DECITIONS OF PARENTHOOD. THOUGH SHE BELONGED TO SUCH AN ORTHODOX SOCIETY SHE HAD A MODERN OUTLOOK. HER MOTHER HAS BEEN PREGNANT FOR ATLEAST 15 TIMES AND HAS MANAGED TO GIVE HEALTHY BIRTH TO ONLY 9 CHILDREN. SEEING THE CONDITION OF HER MOTHERS HEALTH SHE USED TO SUFFER FROM OVER-THINKING AND ANXIETY. WELL, SHE WAS ADMITTED TO A SCHOOL ONLY TILL HER 4TH STANDARD. AFTER THAT LOCALITY PEOPLE ADVISED HER FATHER TO MAKE HER SIT IN THE ROOM AND LEARN SOME HOUSEHOLD CHORES BECAUSE THAT IS ALL WHAT IS EXPECTED FROM HER. WHEN SHE WAS TOLD TO DISCONTINUE THE SCHOOL, SHE WAS

VERY HAPPY OF GETTING RID OF THE POSSIBILITY OF STUDYING. BUT WITHIN FEW MONTHS SHE UNDERTOOD THAT SHE WILL BE LIKE THIS ALL HER LIFE DEPENDING ON HER PARENTS AND WHATEVER BAD OR WORST THEY DECIDE FOR HER. LIMITATIONS ON GOING OUT AND PLAYING STARTED TO POP OUT ONCE SHE REACH THE AGE OF 11. SHE WAS ONLY ALLOWED TO PLAY WITH GIRLS AT THE BACKYARD. THE KIND OF LIFE SHE HAS BEEN SEEN TILL NOW IS LIKE MOTHER WAKES UP EARLY DOES ALL THE WORK. ANYTHING ANYWHERE GOES WRONG HER MOTHER IS BLAMED. HER FATHER AND BROTHERS ENJOY A SUPREME POSITION IN THE FAMILY WHAT EVER THEY NEED IS DONE BY EITHER THE MOTHER OR SISTERS. WIVES HERE ARE EXOECTED TO COOK, CLEAN, LOOK AFTER THE BABY AND ALSO HELP THEIR HUSBAND IN FARMING.

FEW YEARS PASSED LIKE THESE, WHEN NIJU TURNED 14 SOMETHING HAPPENED ON HER BIRTHDAY. HER MOTHER COOKED DELICIOUS MUTTON CURRY, ONION RINGS AND STEAMED RICE WITH BUTTER. SHE WAS COOKING SOME MORE ITEMS THAT NIJU REALLY LIKES BUT SUDDENLY NIJU'S GRANDMA, FATHER CAME IN THE KITCHEN KICKED THE CHULHA AND FEW DISHES WERE ABSOLUTELY SHATTERED AROUND THE KITCHEN FLOOR. NIJU'S MOTHER GOT BEATEN UP BY HER FATHER VERY BADLY. WITHOUT EVEN KNOWING ANYTHING SHE PLEADED FOR HIM TO RELEASE HER. NIJU STARTED TO CRY ALOUD THEN REST OF THE FAMILY RELAXED THE SITUATION. AFTER A WHILE N IJU CAME TO KNOW WHAT HAS HAPPENED! NIJU'S ELDER SISTER MONIKA WAS RETURNING FROM THE MARKET AND WAS STOPPED BY A STRANGER (YOUNG MAN), WHO WAS ASKING FOR SOME DIRECTIONS. THIS WAS SEEN BY SOME OF THE GRAM PANCHAYAT MEMBERS WHO DECIDED TO INFORM HER DAD ABOUT THIS AND TO MARRY HER OFF IMMEDIATELY BECAUSE SHE IS SHAMELESS, SHE CAN DO ANYTHING THAT CAN BE DISRESPECTFULL FOR THE VILLAGE. THE WEDDING TOOK PLACE IN JUST 2 DAYS WITH A KOLKATA BASED BUSINESS MAN. THE DAY OF VIDAY THE HOUSE WAS LEFT ONLY WITH MONIKA'S CLOTHES AND REMINISCENES. THAT NIGHT NIJU THOUGHT THAT WHAT COULD SHE DO TO AVOID SUCH SITUATION? SHE DECIDED ON HERSELF SHE WOULD COMPLETELY RUN AWAY FROM ANY GUY ASKING ANYTHING TO HER.

3 MONTHS PASSEED, ON ONE EVE THE NEWS SURFACED THROUGH THE HOUSE THAT MONIKA IS NOT AT ALL HAPPY WITH HER MARRIAGE

AND HAD A MISCARRIAGE AND STILL HER IN-LAWS ARE NOT ALLOWING HER TO VISIT HER PARENTAL HOUSE. NIJU STRESSED ON THIS AS SHE MISSES HER SISTER VERY MUCH. NIJU'S MOM TOLD HER TO FOCUS ON HER SKIN CARE AND HAIRCARE AS BOY'S FAMILY WILL START TO VISIT THEM WITHIN A WEEK.

THE FIRST ONE SAID YES TO NIJU AND WHY NOT BECAUSE SHE WAS ABSOLUTELY BEAUTIFUL WAIST LENGTH BLACK HAIR, FAIR COMPLEXION BIG SHINNING EYES WITH AN INNOCENT SMILE, SHE WAS AN EASY EXAMPLE OF BONG BEAUTY. THE MARRIAGE TOOK PLACE WITHIN 5 DAYS. THE FAMILY WERE IN A RUSH AS THE GROOM WILL TAKE NIJU TO BANGLADESH. THE MARRIAGE WENT WELL. GREAT ADVICE WERE GIVEN TO NIJU ABOUT PLEASING HIS HUSBAND ON THE WEDDING NIGHT. THE WEDDING NIGHT ARRIVED AND THAT IS WHEN SHE REALISED THAT THINGS DID NOT WATCH HOW SHE WAS TOLD IT WOULD SHE FELT LIKE A BIRD TRAPPED IN A NEST.

SHE TRIED TO SCREAM AND CRY ALOUD BUT THERE WAS NO HOPE. AT DAWN, SHE DICOVERED THAT HE HAS BLEEDED SO THE BEDSHEET IS STAINED. NIJU GETS VERY SCARED AS SHE DOESN'T KNOW ANYTHING ABOUT THE NEW HOUSE AND IT'S WHEREABOUTS. NIJU FINALLY GATHERS THE COURAGE TO CALL HER HUSBAND AND INFORM HIM THE SITUATION. BUT THE HUSBAND CALLED THIS DISTURBING AS TO WHY DID SHE RUIN HIS SLEEP OVER THIS. SHE THEN SOMEHOW MANAGES TROUBLES ONE AFTER THE OTHER BY HER OWN AND HE KEPT ON PRAYING TO GOD, CHANTING RADHEGOBINDO JUST AS HER MOTHER WOULD DO. SHE TOOK BATH IN A PARTITIONED ROOM WITHOUT ROOF, THE KIND OF BATHROOM THEY HAD. SHE TOUCHED HERSELF AS SHE FELT THE BODYACHE, SHE FELT LIKE A FLOWER WHO'S CHASTITY AND PURITY HAS BEEN ABOLISHED. NIJU SUFFERED A LOT IN HIS IN-LAWS HOUSE. RANDOMNLY, SHE GOT BITTEN-UP FROM HER HUSBAND AND MOTHER-IN-LAW. LIFE BECAME A LIVING HELL FOR HER. SHE COULDN'T BEAR IT WHEN HER MOTHER-IN-LAW ALWAYS TRICKED TO MAKE HER THE CULPRIT FOR EVERYTHING. SURPRISINGLY ONE DAY SHE GETS REALLY BITTEN-UP BADLY BY HER HUSBAND AS HE DISCOVERS SHE IS NOT A 10TH PASS. THIS CONTINUED FOR SOME MORE MONTHS BECAUSE OF LACKING IN PROPER NUTRITION SHE STARTED TO LOSE WEIGHT AND LOOK SICK AND TIRED. THE DAY OF JOY CAME IN HER LIFE WHEN SHE DISCOVERS THAT SHE IS PREGNANT! THIS WAS HER BEST CHANCE TO VISIT HER

PARENTAL HOME, NIJU WAS DYING TO SEE HER PARENTS.

SWHE FINALLY GOT HOME AND EMBRACED HER MOTHER, AFTER A WHILE SHE REALIZES THAT HER PARENTS ARE TENSED ABOUT SOMETHING. AFTER NIJU REPEATEDLY ASKED THEM WHAT WAS WRONG THEY SAID HER IN-LAWS HAS DEMANDED 200 GRAMS OF GOLD IF SHE IS UNABLE TO BEAR A BOY CHILD, NIJU HAS BEEN ASKED NOT TO RETURN IN HER IN-LAWS UNTIL SHE DELIVERS!

THIS WAS THE FIRST TIME IN NIJU'S LIFE THAT SHE FELT SHE WAS NOT ATALL WELCOMED IN HER OWN HOME. HER GRANDMA STARTED TO SAY THINGS LIKE WHY WOULD YOU WANT TO VISIT US? YOU ARE THE REASON OF THEIR DISTURBED MIND AND NATURE. HELPLESS NIJU LOOKED AT HER MOTHER BUT EVEN HER MOTHER DID NOT TAKE ANY STAND FOR HER, SHE ALSO BHAD HEADACHES ABOUT THE OTHER TWO DAUGHTER'S MARRIAGE AND THEIR DOWRY!

THE 15 YEAR OLD COULDN'T UNDERSTAND WHAT IS GOING ON IN HER LIFE! SHE SPENDED MOST OF HER TIMES CHANTING PRAYERS, DOING LIGHT HOUSEHOLD WORKS AND SPENDING TIME WITH HER SIBLINGS. FINALLY, THE DAY COMES AND SHE DELIVERS HER BABY BOY. SHE WAS SO HAPPY TO HOLD HER BABY FOR THE VERY FIRST TIME, BUT SHE HAD A C-SECTION DELIVERY DUE TO SOME COMPLICATIONS. THE NEWS SURFACED AND PEOPLE STARTED TO COMMENT ON HER DELIVERY SAYING: 'THIS WAS An EASY WAY TO GIVE BIRTH, SHE DIDN'T EVEN BEAR THE LABOUR THEN HOW CAN SHE BE A GOOD MOTHER, SHE JUST ENTERENED MOTHERHOOD JUST LIKE THAT!'

ALL THESE TORTURED NIJU, SHE COULDN'T IGNORE ALL OF THEM. SHE RETURNED TO HER IN-LAWS. SHE FELT THEY WERE HAPPY ABOUT THE BABY BOY. BUT, AS THE DAYS PASSED OLD TOTURES BEGAN A ND SHE COULDN'T EVEN PROPERLY FEED HER BABY, THE BABY TURNED OUT TO BE VERY GOOD LIKE, JUST LIKE HER MOTHER BUT NIJU COULDN'T PROVIDE EVEN EDUCATION TO HIM. SHDE GAVE UP ON LIFE. DAYS WOULD PASS SHE WONT COOK AS THERE WOULD BE ONLY STEAM RICE TO RICE OR PUFFED RICE, NOT EVEN POTATO OR LENTIL. SHE SAW HOW HER IN-LAWS SEPARETED THEM IN OUTHOUSE AND THEY LIVED IN SUCH HARMONY. A WOMAN STARTED VISITING THEIR HOME WITH NIJU'S HUSBAND. NIJU DOUBTED THAT TWO ARE IN A RELATIONSHIP. SHE NAMED HER SON LAKSYA, SHE WAS SURPRISED TO SEE THAT HER IN -LAWS DIDN'T EVEN LOVED LAKSYA. LAKSYA WAS ADORED BY THEIR VILLAGE PEOPLE THEIR HOUSE WAS ON RIVER-SIDE

AT BANGLADESH.

OFTEN THEIR NEIGHBOUR WOULD ASK LAKSYA WHAT DID YOU HAVE IN LUNCH? AND THE BABY BOY WITHOUT KNOWING THE CRUELTY OF REALITY WOULD REPLY IN INNOCENSE SAYING MY MOTHER DIDN'T COOK TODAY! EVERYDAY SOMEONE FROM THE NEIGHBOURHOOD WOULD FEED LAKSYA. ONE DAY, NIJU'S FATHER TRILOKESH ALONG WITH HER BIG BROTHER NIKHILESH (NIKHIL) WOULD VISIT HER HOUSE TO CHECK ON HER AND BROUGHT A BAG FULL OF SEASONAL FRUIT MANGO A BIG HILSA FISH AND SWEET CURD IN A RED EARTHEN POT AS OFFERING TO HER IN-LAWS. NIJU'S IN-LAWS WERE NOT PLEASED TO SEE HER PARENTS. NIJU BURST OUT INTO TEARS AND SAID EVERYTHING TO HER PARENTS REQUESTING THEM TO TAKE HER ALONG WITH THEM. NIJU'S FATHER ABOUT HER HUSBAND'S AFFAIR AS HE WAS WALKING IN THE HOUSE WITH HIS GIRLFRIEND WITHOUT KNOWING THAT HIS IN-LAWS ARE RIGHT PRESENT OVER THERE! THOUGH TRILOKESH WAS REALLY NOT INTERESTED IN TALKING BACK HIS DAUGHTER BUT LOOKING AT HIS GRANDCHILD'S FACE HE WAS CONFUSED. AT THIS POINT, NIKHIL TOOK A STAND FOR NILANJANA AND ASKED HIS FATHER TO TAKE NIJU BACK WITH THEM.

A YEAR PASSED AWAY, SHE WAS 17, HUSBAND-LESS, HAD AN ILLETERATE CHILD, BEING A BURDEN FOR THE FAMILY NIJU WENT INTO SERIOUS DEDPRESSION. MONTHS PASSED AND ONE DAY HER GRANDMA DIED. PATRIORCHAL RULES SEEMED TO BE RELAXED A BIT SINCE THEN. LAKSYA WAS ADMITTED TO SCHOOL BY NIKHIL. NIJU REMAINED BUSY WITH OTHER HOUSE HOLD CHORES WITH HER MOTHER AS NONE OF HER BROTHERS WERE MARRIED BY THEN.

YEARS PASSED, ONE BY ONE HER BROTHERS GOT MARRIED. EVERYONE BEHAVED WITH HER IN A RUDE WAY. SHE WAS AS IF OF NO VALUE. WHEN LAKSYA GOT PROMOTED TGO CLASS 10 NIJU'S FAMILY DECIDED TO STOP LAKSYA FROM GOING TO SCHOOL AS THE EXPENSES OF THE FAMILY GOT VERY HIGH AFTER HER BROTHERS ALSO HAD CHILDREN. NIJU WAS UNDER SHOCK SHE THOUGHT FOR A MINUTE THAT THERE WAS NO WAY SHE COULD BEAR THE COST OF HIS STUDIES SHE DOESN'T HAVE AN SKILL TO WORK, DOESN'T HAVE ANY JEWELLARY TO SALE EITHER. SHE PLEADED TO HER MOTHER, REQUESTED HER BROTHER'S WIVES THAT SHE WOULD WORK HARD DO THEIR PART OF THE WORK AS WELL BUT JUST TO ATLEAST LET

LAKSYA COMPLETE HIS 10TH. THEY AGREED, LAKSYA SECURED A GOOD MARKS AND SOON AFTER STARTED TO DO SOME FARMING JOBS FOR THE FAMILY. SUDDENLY, ONE DAY LAKSYA FATHER VIPIN VISITED THEIR HOME. BEING THE JAMAI, GROOMS ALWAYS ENJOYED A SENSE OF ATTENTION IN EVERY FAMILY NO MATTER WHAT. HE CONVINCED NIJU TO COME ALONG WITH HIM TO BRINDABAN WHERE HE HAS STARTED THE JOB OF A TOUR GUIDE. NIJU BID GOODBYE TO HER FAMILY AND WENT OFF TO BRINDABAN WITH SON AND HUSBAND.

AFTER 2 YEARS SHE REALIZED SHE HAS AGAIN BEEN FOOLED BY HER HUSBAND AS HE HAS LEFT BRINFABAN AND WENT TO BANGLADESH WITHOUT INFORMING HER. SHE REMAINED AS A MAID FOR TWO YEARS DOING ALL THE WORK AND LAKSYA WOULD ALSO WORK FOR PART-TIME JOBS TO SUPPORT THE FAMILY, QUITTING HIS STUDIES. THIS SMALL NUCLEAR FAMILY WAS LIKE A BLISS TO THEM.BUT, THEIR DREAM CAME OUT TO BE FALSE. DISHEARTEDNED THEY THOUGHT NOT TO RETURN TO BONGAON EITHER. MOTHER AND SON WHO HAS ALWAYS BEEN THE CENTRE OF HATRED AND DISRESPECT THOUGHT TO NOT BEG TO ANYONE THIS TIME. NOW THEBIG QUESTION WAS WHAT TO DO WHO WILL PAY THE RENT, BILLS EVERYTHING? THAT'S WHEN LAKSYA STARTED TO WORK DAYA ND NIGHT TO RUN THE FAMILY. NILANJANA ACCIDENTLY FELT VERY SICK HER RIGHT FOOT SWELLED UP AND SHE PRACTICALLY COULDN'T DO ANYTHING. ALL THE HOUSEHOLD CHORES WERE MANAGED BY LAKSYA ITSELF. THIS WENT ON FOR SOME MORE MONTHS AND LAKSYA FELT SICK SEVERELY. THEY RETUJRNED TO BONGAON, SAME OLD LIFE, LAKSYA STARTED TO WORK ON FIELDS. NIJU REMAINED BUSY COOKING, WASHING AND CLEANING. VIPIN STARTED TO VISIT THEM OFTEN EVERYTIME IN NEW ATTIRE AS A COSTUME SHOW. NIJU'S FAMILY REPEATEDLY ASKED VIPIN TO TAKE NILANJANA ALONG WITH HIM TO BANGLADESH BUT HE REFUSED. AT THIS POINT, NILANJANA THOUGH AWARE OF THE SITUATION TRIED NOT TO TRUST HIM AGAIN BUT ENDED UP AGAIN DREAMING OF A NORMAL FAMILY. THIS WAS GOING QUITE WELL ONLY WHEN VIPIN AGAIN VANISHED. THE GOT TO KNOWS GTHE MAN WAS A COMPLETE FRAUD RENTED FROM MANY PLACES AND HAS FINALLY FLEED AWAY TO BANGLADESH. NIJU DEEP DOWN JUST FELT THAT VIPIN LOVES HIM, WHAT COULD SHE ANYWAYS THINK? AFTERALL VIPIN IS THE ONLY PERSON SHE HAS LOVED ALL HER LIFE.

ON ONE FINE EVE VIPIN CALLS ON THEIR LANDLINE NO. AND SAYS THAT HE HAS MARRIED ANOTHER GIRL AND HAS STARTED A NEW LIFE. NIJU BREAKED IN TO PIECES AFTER THIS. NIKHIL BRINGS NIJU AND LAKSYA TO KOLKATTA HELPS LAKSYA TO RUN HIS BUSINESS AS A STARTUP AND HELP THEM TO GET A SMALL RENTED FLAT. NIJU WAS NOW ON HER EARLY 40'S , SHE NOW DREAMT OF JUST A NORMAL FAMILY WITH SON , DAUGHTER-IN-LAW AND GRANDCHILDREN. BUT, SOON SHED FACED THE REALITY HER SON LAKSYA WHO HAPPENED TO BE SO NICE HAS CHANGED A LOT! HE NOW WANTED TO GET RID OF HIS MOTHER AND SEE SEVERAL GIRFLS BRIN G THEM ON FLAT AND ENJOY HIS LIFE. SOON AFTER HIS MOTHER NIJU SENSED HIS INTENTIONS SHE FORCED HIM TO GET MARRIED. LAKSYA HAD A GIRLFRIEND CALLED RUPA. THEY GOT MARRIED SECRETLY WITHOUT INFORMING THE WHOLE FAMILY, TOOK AWAY ALL OF NIJU'S GOLDS AND ASKED HER TO GO B ACK TO BONGAON. NIJU PRFOTESTED BUT ALL HER EFFORT WENT IN TO VAIN AND SOON SHE WAS SENT BACK TO BONGAON. WHILE SHE RETURNED TO HER HOME THIS TIME HER POSITION WAS WAY WORST THAN EVER AS SHE EARNED THE TAG OF A BAD MOTHER-IN-LAW TOO. PEOPLE STARTED TO JUDGE HER SAYING THINGS LIKE NEITHER WITH HUSBAND NOR WITH SON SHE COULD ADJUST. NILANJANA WAS NOW FACING DEPRESSION AND SHE PRACTICALLY STOPPED DOING ALL THE POSITIVE THINGS IN HER LIFE. SOON AFTER, SHE GOT THE NEWS THAT SHE WAS A GRANDMOTHER NOW AS HER DAUGHER-IN-LAW GAVE BIRTH TO A BABY GIRL, DESPITE THE BITTER RELATION NIJU CONGRATULATED RUPA. RUPA IN RETURN INSULTED HER BY SAYING NIJU COULDN'T UPBRING HER SON WELL, RUPA COMPLINED THAT WHILE SHE WAS PREGNANT LAKSYA WAS DATING OTHER GIRLS. EVERY TIME SHE CAUGHTS HIM RED-HANDED. HEARING ALL THESE DEEP DOWN, NIJU KNEW THAT RUPA WAS NOT LYING, SHE FELT BAD ABOUT RUPA AS LAKSYA HAS STARTED ACTING LIKE HIS DAD. NILANJANA ASKED RUPA THAT I AM MILES AWAY HERE, WHAT CAN I DO ABOUT THE SITUATION? I AM THAT UNFORTUNATE LADY WHO IS BEEN KICKED OUT BY HER OWN SON. YOU ARE HIS WIFE, HIS SOUL-MATE.THEN STOP THINKING ABOUT GIVING UP AND TRY TO MAKE MY SON A BETTER PERSON FOR YOU.

THIS CONTINUED FOR MORE THAN 3 YEARS. SOMETIMES RUPA MIGHT CALL NILANJANA TO SHOUT AND ARGUE AN D SOMETIMES LAKSYA CALLED TO TALK ABOUT LENDING MONEY AND PROPERTY.

UNTIL ONE DAY WHEN IN 3 YEARS LAKSYA CAME TO VISIT NIJU TO INFORM THAT HE HAD A DIVORCE. HE APOLOGIZED TO HIS MOTHER. LAKSYA BROUGHT HIS MOTHER BACK TOOK A NEW RENTAL APARTMENT AND STARTING LIVING THERE. NIJU DISCOVERED THAT LAKSYA HAS GROWN HIS BUSINESS REALLY BIG BUT HAS DEVELOPED VERY BITTER RELATION WITH NIKHILESH AND FEW OTHERS OF THEIR FAMILY.

NIJU NEVER BROUGHT BACK ANY OLD TOPIC AS SHE WANTED HIM TO MOVE ON AND LEAD A BETTER LIFE. SOME TIMES TOXIC PEOPLE AROUND THEM WOULD TAUNT LAKSYA BUT NIJU ALWAYS ACTED WITH PATIENCE AND NEVER REACTED. 9 MONTHS PASSED LIKE THIS ONLY WHEN NIJU ONCE REALIZED THAT ALL HER DOCUMENTS, ADDRESS PROOF AND IDENTITY DOCUMENTS ALL ARE GONE. SHE WAITED FOR LAKSYA TO RETURN FROM WORK. LAKSYA RETURNED FROM HOME AROUND 9 AT NIGHT. NIJU ASKED HIM ABOUT THE DOCUMENTS. LAKSYA THOUGHT FOR A MOMENT AND SAID THAT I CANNOT D=FIND MY FOUR-WHEELER DOCUMENTS AND LICENCE TOO. LET ME CALL RUPA AND ASK! LATER THE NEXT DAY MORNING, LAKSYA INFORMS HIS MOTHER THAT SHE HAS INTENTIONALLY TAKEN AWAY ALL THE PAPERS. SHE IS ASKING LAKSYA TO PAY OFF THE ALIMONY OUT OF COURT. LAKSYA ASKED NIJU TO WAIT FOR SOME MORE DAYS.

DAYS PASSEED AND THINGS WENT ON LIKE THE SAME. THEIR 2BHK APARTMENT WAS GRTTING FILLED WITH SECOND HAND FURNITURES AND LAKSYA ALSO BOUGHT MICROWAVE AND REFRIGARETOR FOR THE KITCHEN. THEY NOW HAD A 32 INCH SMART TV IN THEIR LIVING CUM DINNING ROOM.

NIJU WOULD SPENT ALL HER TIME READING THE HOLY BOOKS, COOKING DISHES, CLEANING HOUSE, WATCHING TV AND WASHING ENDLESS CLOTHES.

YES, WASHING ENDLESS CLOTHES BECAUSE THEY ALSO HAD A PART BUSINESS OF DRY CLEANING. SO YES, THOSE CLOTHES WERE WASHED AT HOME USING SOME CHEMICALS. THIS WENT ON FOR ANOTHER 2 YEARS. THEN NILANJANA SUFFERED WITH HER HAND AS THE SKIN STARTED REACTING BECAUSE OF THE CHEMICALS. SHE CONSUKTED DOCTOR AND WAS ASKED TO TAKE FULL BED REST. THAT BIS WHEN IT STRIKED LAKSYA THAT HE SHOULD HAVE THOUGHT ABOUT A DOMESTIC HELP EARLIER. HE QUICKLY ASSIGNED A PERSON WHO'S NAME WAS PARUL TO HELP HIS MA. PARUL DID ALL THE HOUSEHOLD

WORKS. PARUL WAS THE SAME AGE AS WAS LAKYSA. SOMETIMES SHE WOULD WATCH A WEB SERIIES WITH NIJU OR HEAR STORIES ABOUT NIJU'S PAST LIFE. NIJU GRADUALLY GOT BETTER AND RETURNED TO HER FORM BUT THE CHEMICAL WASHING WAS STOPPED FOR HER. LAKSYA APPOINTED TWO MORE BOYS FOR THE TASK.

SEEING LAKSYA SOMETIMES NIJU FELT VERY GOOD. MOTHER AND SON SAW A LOT IN LIFE BUT FINALLY THEY ARE HAVING A PEACEFUL LIFE! IN THE MONTH OF JANUARY,2018 THEY WERE INVITED FOR NIKHILESH'S ELDER SON'S MARRIAGE. SHE WAS REALLY HAPPY

TO REUNITE WITH THE FAMILY BUT HAD NO IDEA ON WHAT SHE SHOULD GIFT TO NIKHILESH'S DAUGHTER IN LAW. SHE THEN QUICKLY TOOK OUT THE ONLY PAIR OF GOLD BANGLES SHE WAS LEFT WITH, SHE LOOKED AT THEM VERY CAREFULLY AND ASKED LAKSYA TO TAKE THEM FOR POLISHING. LAKSYA PROTESTED SEEEING THIS, HE SAID I CANNOT AFFORD GIVING GOLD PRESENT TO THEM MA! AND YOU ARE ONLY LEFT WITH THIS WHAT WILL YOU GIVE WHEN REST OF THE BROTHERS WILL GET MARRIED. NIJU FALLED SILENT. LAKSYA THEN SUGGESTED HIS MOM TO BUY A GOOD SAREE FOR THE BRIDE.

THEN, AFTER FEW DAYS THE MARRIAGE TOOK PLACE AND NIJU WAS REUNITED WITH HER FAMILY. SHE WAS VERY HAPPY TO BE AROUND HER FAMILY.

2020 MARCH, THE MONTH PANDEMIC BREAKED OUT IN KOLKATA. IT GOT REALLY WORST FOR ALL! LAKSYA'S IRON BUSINESS AND DRY-CLEANING BUSINESS GOT SHUT. HE NOW ONLY RELIED ON WATER SUPPLY AND RAPIDO. YES, RAPIDO IS THE BIKE-TAXI APP. NILANJANA WOULD SPEND HER DAYS IN MISERY THINKING ABOUT LAKSYA AS HE RIDED HIS BIKE DAY AND NIGHT WITHOUT LICENSE AND PROPER SAFETY. TWICE HE HAS FACED ACCIDENT. NILANJANA DISCOVERED THAT THE URGE OF INCOMING SO MUCH OF MOEY IS NOT BECAUSE OF RUNNING THIS HOUSE BUT TO RUN ANOTHER HOUSE THAT HE HAS DEVELOPED FOR HIM. HE ALSO WAS STAYING IN A LIVING RELATION WITH A GIRL 2 YEARS ELDER THAN HIS AGE HAVING 3 CHILDREN. THE WOMAN'S NAME WAS PARUL! THE DOMESTIC HELPING MAID OF THEIR HOUSE. NILANJANA GOT TO KNOW ALL THESE FROM THE LITTLE HELPING BOY OF LAKSYA'S WATER SUPPLYING BUSINESS. SHE CALLED UP LAKSYA AND SAID A LOT OF BITTER WORDS EXPRESSING ALL HER WORRIES AND FRUSTRATION.

IT WAS NOT TOO LATE AFTER THIS THAT LAKSYA COMPLETELY STOPPED VISITING HIS MA, EVEN STOPPED BUYING NECESITIES FOR HER. SHE RUN OUT OF MEDICINE AND FOOD. SOMETIMES LAKYA WOULD SEND HER BACK TO BONGAON BUT, EVEN THERE PEOPLE WERE IRRITATED TO SEE HER AND LOOK AFTER HER. SHE IN HER KOLKATA FLAT WOULD REMAIN HUNGRY FOR DAYS WAITING FOR LAKSYA TO COME. SOMETIMES SHE CALLED UP SOME OF HER WELL WISHERS IN THE FAMILY TO CALL UP LAKSYA AND ASK HIM TO GET HER SOME GROCERIES. THINGS WENT WORST WHEN THE FLAT WHERE SHE WAS LIVING IN, THE LAND LADY ASKED HER TO LEAVE THE APARTMENT AS SHE WISHED TO SALE IT. SHE HAD NO BALANCE IN HER MOBILE PHONE SO SHE KEPT ON GIVING MIST CALLS TO LAKSYA UNTIL HE CALLED BACK. HEAFRING EVERYTHING LAKSYA SAID THAT FINE YOU COME IN OUR APARTMENT AND STAY WITH US. NILANJANA REPLIED IN IRRITATION THAT IF IT WAS HIS MARRIED WIFE SHE WOULD HAVE COME ALONG BUT SHE WAS A MAID WITH

CHILDREN HE WAS LIVING WITH. THE FINAL DAY ARRIVED WHEN SHE WAS ASKED TO LEAVE THE FLAT. FOR THE LAST TIME SHE CALLED UP NIKHILESH ONLY THAT LAKSYA TOOK PARUL TO SEVERAL PLACES AND WAS UNDER THE RAID OF THE POILCE EVERYTIME HE ESPACED USING NIKHILESH'S NAME. THEY WERE MAD AT NIJU AND HER SON. SHE CALLED AT BONGAON TO KNOW LAKSYA ALSO HAS SEVERAL RELATIONS WITH SOME GIRLS THERE AND HAS ALSO SLEPT WITH THEM. LAKSYA WAS FULLY SCANDALIZED OVER THERE.

NILANJANA WENT SILENT FOR 5 MINS, SHE SAT ON A SOFA PRACTICALLY DOING NOTHING. SHE DRANK SOME OF THE WATER FROM THE BOTTLE BESIDE HER BED AND DECIDED ON DOING SOMETHING COMPLETE DIFFERENT FROM HER PERSONALITY. SHE TOOK OUT THOSE TWO BANGLES WENT TO THE JEWELLARY SHOP TO SELL THEM. SHE GOT 70,000 SELLING THEM. SHE CAME BACK TOOK 5 THOUSAND AND WENT TO THE LAND LADY ASKED HER TO CONSIDER HER FOR 15 MORE DAYS IN RETUR SHE WOULD PAY DOUBLE THE RENT. THE LAND LADY THOUGHT FOR A MOMENT AND AGREED TO HER PROPOSAL.IN THE EVENING SHE WENT OUT TO THE LOCAL MARKET PURCHASED 5 UNIFORM SAREES AND BOUGHT SOME GROCERIES. LATER THAT NIGHT AFTER HAVING DINNER SHE THOUGHT ABOUT HER PLANS THE NEXT DAY AND WENT OFF TO SLEEP PEACEFULLY. THE VERY NEXT DAY SHE PLANNED TO VISIT URBANNA A BIG HOUSING

NEXT TO HER FLAT TO TALK WITH THEM REGARDING COOKING WORK, BUT SHE NEEDED AN ACCESS TO GET UP. SO, SHE USED HER CONTACT SUDIPA A WOMAN OF HER AGE SHE KNEW FROM THE LOCALITY. SHE CALLED UP SUDIPA AND ASKED IF SHE CAN COME OVER. SUDIPA THOUGH FELT AWKARD BUT STILL SAID YES. REACHING THERE SHE CAME TO KNOW THAT SUDIPA DOES ALL HER CHORES ALONE AS DOCTOR HAS SUGEESTED HER TO HVE A LOT OF PHYSICAL ACTIVITIES. BUT, SHE SAID NIJU THAT I CAN CHECK WITH MY SON AND DAUGHTER-IN-LAW AS THEY ARE BOTH WORKING PROFFESIONALS THEY NEEDS DOMESTIC HELP VERY BADLY. AS ALL THE MAIDS ARE GONE FOR THIS LOCKDOWN. WITHIN AN HOUR EVERYTHING WAS SET.

SUDIPA'S SON AND DAUGHTER-IN-LAW WERE EDITORS AND SUPER BUSY WORKING COUPLE AMAYRA AND AKASH DIDN'T HAVE ANY CHILD AND WAS LOOKING FOR A LADY WHO WOULD ALL THE CHORES STAYING WITH THEM IN THE MAID'S ROOM. NIJU AGREED TO EVERYTHING THEY OFFEREDC HER A SALARY OF 12 THOUSAND. NILANJANA COULDN'T BELIEVE HER EARS. SHE WENT BACK TO HER APARTMENT PACKED HER CLOTHES IN A SUITCASE TOOK HERS GODS HOME TEMPLE AND HOLY BOOKS IN ANOTHER SUITCADSE AND LEFT THE FLAT. SHE MOVED IN URBANNA. SHE CALLED UP LAKSYA JUST TO INFORM THAT HE CAN TAKE AWAY ALL THE FURNITURES AND ELECTRICAL APPLIANCES IF HE WANTED TO. THAT WAS THE LAST YTIME SHE SPOKE TO LAKSYA. SHE BREAKED HER SIM CARD AND THREWB INTO TRASH. WITHING FEW DAYS SHE GOT A NEW SIM CARD AND OPENED A BANK ACCOUNT TO DEPOSIT HER CASH . WITHIN ONE MONTH, SHE BOUGHT AN ANDROID PHONE SO THAT SHE CAN LISTEN TO HOLY SONGS WHILE DOING WORKS. ONE DAY SHE WAS RETURNING FROM THE MARKET AND SHE NOTICED HERSELF IN THE LIFT MIRROR AND WAS AMAZED AT THE BEAUTY OF HER THIS NEW LIFE, NOT DEPENDING UPON ANYONE, NOT BOWING TO ANYONE SHE FELT SHE WAS REBORN. SHE ALWAYS CHANTED PRAYERS AND THANKED HER SEVERAL GODS FOR GIVING HER SO MUCH OF STRENGH. SHE DIDN'T LOOK BACK AT HER FAMILY TILL DATE AS SHE KNEW THE KIND OF PATRIORCHAL FAMILY SHE CAME FROM WOULD NEVER ACCEPT HER NEW NEW LIFE. SHE CONTINUED TO WORK THER AFTER 3 MONTHS OF JOINING HERE SHE BOUGHT A STICHING MACHINE AND STARTED TO STITCH FOR THE HOUSING PEOPLE AND MAKE A GOOD AMOUNT OF EXTRA MONEY IN A MONTH.

ONCE AMAYRA ASKED HER THAY WHERE DID SHE LEARNED STICHING FROM NIJU SMILED AND SAID YOUTUBE. AMAYRA AND AKSASH WOULD ALWAYS SUPPORT HER AS SHE DID ALL THE CHORES OF THE HOUSEHOLD SINGLE-HANDEDLY AND STILL MANAGED TO OVER-WORK. AT THE END OF THE YEAR 2021, SHE LEFT URBANNA AND SHIFTED TO A 2BHK RENTED APARTMENT AT A NEARBY LOCATION AND STARTED HER NEW BUSINESS OF A CLOUD KITCHEN. SHE STILL CONTINUED TO WORK FOR AMAYRA ONLY FOR THE COOKING PART. AS THEY GAVE BIRTH TO A BEAUTIFUL DAUGHTER AND THEY NEEDED A 24/7 BABY SITTER BUT THEY CAN'T THINK OF HAVING FOOD ANYWHERE ELSE.

NILANJANA NOW HANDLES HER CLOUD KITCKEN, TAILORING BUSINEES AND COOKING JOB ALL TOGETHER. AS MUCH AS I HAVE SEEN IN MY LIFE SHE IS THE MOST STRONG SINGLE MULTI-TASTKING FEARLESS WOMAN I HAVE EVER MET.

THIS IS NOT A FICTIONAL STORY, THEN WHO AM I?

I AM HER NEIGHBOUR, JUST THOUGHT TO PEN DOWN HER LIFESTORY, LEAVING THE REST UPTO MY READERS.

SOUMILI PAUL.

NOW THAT I HVE COME TO THE END OF MY STORY I WOULD TELL ALL MY READERS THAT SHE IS A STRONG LADY NOW. SHE WOULD BE REALLY HAPPY TO KNOW THAT SOMEONE ACTUALLY READ HER LIFE-STORY. CONTINUE SUPPORTING ME LIKE THIS. LOVE YOU.